CONSUMING FIRE
A JOURNEY OF HEALING
TRAUMA'S DEEP HURTS

A COMPANION FOR
DAVE ROEVER'S
FORGED IN FIRE

REAP INTERNATIONAL PUBLICATION
PEGGY CORVIN
CO-AUTHOR

So be truly glad.

*There is wonderful joy ahead, even though you must
endure many trials for a little while.*

These trials will show that your faith is genuine.

*It is being tested as fire tests and purifies gold—though
your faith is far more precious than mere gold.*

*So when your faith remains strong through
many trials, it will bring you much praise and glory
and honor on the day when Jesus Christ is revealed to
the whole world.*

1 Peter 1

CONTENTS

INTRODUCTION

Forged In Fire excerpt:

"Becoming Dave Roever,
the man of God
I was created to be,
while living in the scarred body
war had given birth to,
was one of the most difficult
challenges of my life.
Some days brought me to my
knees as I fought through
self-criticism and self-doubt."

In his powerful book, *Forged In Fire: The Roever Family Story,* Dave Roever transparently shared the heartbreak, despair, strength, and victory he and his family encountered in the aftermath of tremendous trauma.

He experienced trauma in a war-torn country at the hands of an enemy. In this world, there are many sources of trauma. This guidebook is for all who have suffered at the hands of trauma.

From battlefields, school yards, sports fields, and living rooms that have become dying rooms, we hear and see the resultant suffering. Yet, the torment and lasting bitterness hide deep in the hearts and minds of those who never deserved what happened to them.

Throughout Scripture, we see the desire of God's heart is simply to have us be His people who choose Him to be our God so He can come and live among us. That is the very image of life in Eden, and it is the vision of the New Jerusalem revealed as our future hope.

God is frequently portrayed as using fire to burn away everything that is not of Him. He is a consuming fire that takes the dark, unholy, evil, harmful things and burns them.

As followers of Jesus, our salvation is secure, and our future is set. We will be with Him in the New Jerusalem. That is good news, but He has more for us.

When there is trauma in life, shadows can be cast into our souls to keep us from knowing God intimately so He can live with us now. He wants to send His Spirit to burn up all those painful remnants and restore our closeness with Him.

So often, when we are involved in trauma, it leaves pain so deep that we feel it will overwhelm us. It can also leave a sense of guilt and shame that we are reluctant to discuss. Those secrets keep us stuck in a repeating pattern of self-defeating behavior. Just like Adam and Eve, we think we have to hide from God.

God invites us to let Him rule in our life so He can heal the hurt, restore our thinking, and save our lives from the destruction that seems to loom ahead.

All that is required of us is to call on His name and accept His invitation.

This is an invitation to reach inside where your courage lives and face the lies, limitations, and labels that want to rob you of your joy! Come, take back your soul.

PART 1

BEGINNING

FORGED IN FIRE EXCERPT:

"I was in the hospital for a year and two months, and it was a great blessing to be able to then walk out with my suitcase in one hand and my sweetheart in the other."

This line from Dave's book poignantly illustrates the moment when his life focus shifted. He had suffered the trauma, endured the treatments, and lived in an environment focused on healing his body. Now it was time to start again. The next chapter of his life would be to seek out healing for the hidden wounds.

The world we live in is a broken place filled with broken people. One common reaction to what we see and experience is to blame God and condemn the broken people who have broken our hearts and, frequently, our bodies. The longer we live with that mindset, the more isolated we become and the more hopeless our world can seem.

The purpose of this study guide is to discover, define, and defeat anything that is keeping you from becoming the fullness of the person God created you to be. Are you ready to start again with a focus on healing? Since He made you, only He can truly heal and restore you.

The mission of this study guide is to bring you closer to Him by encouraging you to open your spiritual eyes to see Him in a new way and to open your spiritual ears so you can hear Him more clearly than ever.

Are you close to God? Do you know how close He is to you? His word in Psalm 34:18 declares, "The Lord is near to those who have a broken heart. And He saves those who are broken in spirit." Many people who have suffered deep pain because of trauma are brokenhearted and have a broken spirit. God is near because that is not what He desired for His creation. He is near because He wants a close relationship with you. He is near because He has the power to heal your hurt and restore your joy. He is near because He loves you.

Your closeness to God, however, can be limited by your beliefs about Him. You may be angry with Him, or you may see Him as distant and unapproachable, or perhaps you see Him as angry at you. This is an invitation to consider Him anew; perhaps there is more to Him than you have ever understood. This guide uses prayer and Scripture to help you draw closer.

Prayer is crucial. Prayer is the mode of transportation for this entire journey. If you want to draw closer to God, spend time talking to Him and spend more time listening to Him. "What do you want to say to me?" is a valid question when you are seeking God. Prayer requires time to sit, sometimes in silence, until you hear from God. Jesus said, "My sheep know my voice." Are you listening?

Scripture is God's autobiography. He prompted about 40 people to write down the message He wanted to tell all of eternity. Billy Graham used the words from the Bible to draw people to Jesus. He spoke in person to over 215 million people. Using media, he was heard by 2.2 billion people and saw over 2 million respond to his invitation. Because he saw lives change, in his book, *Peace with God: The Secret of Happiness,* he wrote, "The very practice of reading the Bible will have a purifying effect upon your mind and heart. Let nothing take the place of this daily exercise."

Where do you begin? Always in prayer, often by saying, "God, I need your help to fully understand what you are saying in your Word to me today." He is faithful to help.

SCRIPTURE STUDY:
WHAT IS GOD LIKE?

Deuteronomy 9:1-3

Zechariah 13:8-9; and 2:5

Matthew 3:11

Hebrews 12:28-29

1 Peter 1:3-7

Focus: *Consuming Fire*

God is holy. None of us are. Yet, His entire design is for us to live in a peaceful world with Him.

These Scriptures showed many ways He uses fire to achieve that desire. He destroyed enemies, purified His children, and set a wall of fire around them to keep evil away. Jesus baptizes us with the Holy Spirit and fire to burn off all that is not of God. God wants to burn off the effects of trauma in our lives. Spend time in prayer asking what is in your life that God wants to consume so He can restore you and deepen your relationship with Him.

HEARTWORK

After prayer and time in the presence of God, write out what He has shown you.

Discover

What have you found that needs to be removed from your life?

Do you have sin or perhaps spiritual laziness? Are you clinging to the role of victim? Perhaps you have negative friends and influences that are harmful. Are you willing to seek better influences for your soul?

Define

How does each one on your list keep you from having a close relationship with Jesus?

Many times, we are bound by lies about God. Look at this list to see if you agree with any of these:

List of Common Lies

He doesn't love me	He caused my problems
He is angry with me and	He could have changed
He wants to punish me	things but didn't.
I'm not special	
I don't deserve His love	

Defeat

What keeps you from letting Him in so that He can purify your heart from each one?

Ask Him what His truth is about each thing above.

Be willing to believe Him.

ONE VICTOR'S VOICE
WHAT'S IN YOUR SUITCASE?

I have always known about God. Every time I heard Him called "God the Father," I just got madder. When I would hear people say the "Lord's Prayer," which Jesus started with "Our Father," I would harden my heart against Jesus even more.

With every new form of abuse and trauma delivered by the hands of my earthly father, I compiled another testimony against this heavenly father and added it to my case. I soon had a suitcase of anger and bitterness and lugged it everywhere I went. Because I was so angry and bitter, I drove everyone around me out of my life. Each broken relationship proved to me that since God didn't love me, no one else ever would.

Then I met Jesus. I wasn't looking for Him; He just waded into my darkness and told me He loved me. No one had ever told me that. I believed Him because somewhere in me, I knew it was true. Thankfully He was patient with me, so bit by bit, as I unpacked all that I was carrying in that suitcase, He healed my heart.

He sent His Spirit to me and began showing me the Father. Now I know He isn't some distant, angry father; I know Him as Abba who loves me. The amazing thing is that now, He is showing me how much He likes me, too. That gives me courage.

Have you invited Jesus into your heart to be your Lord and Savior?

Perhaps you related to this account of another person's journey. You don't have to wait until you get to church to invite Jesus to be your Lord and Savior. It is important for you to know that He is ready and willing and will meet you where ever you are. If you are serious about healing from your past, you need a personal relationship with Him. Consider these Scriptures:

"For by grace you have been saved through faith, and that not of yourselves; it is the gift of God, not of works, lest anyone should boast." Ephesians 2: 8-9

"For God so loved the world that He gave His only begotten Son, that whoever believes in Him should not perish but have everlasting life. For God did not send His Son into the world to condemn the world, but that the world through Him might be saved. "He who believes in Him is not condemned, but he who does not believe is condemned already because he has not believed in the name of the only begotten Son of God." John 3:16-18

If you want to accept Him as your Savior, pray these things to Him from your heart.

Jesus, I confess that I have sinned against You. Please forgive me. I repent from sin and open my heart to You. Will you come into my life to be my Lord and Savior? I give You my life and ask that You take it and help me learn how to serve you from this day forward.

Lord, I believe you have come into my heart and forgiven me of all my sins. Thank you for saving me.

Lord, will You fill me with Your Holy Spirit and give me the power to change, to know You, and to live every day for You? I need you, Jesus. Amen!

If you prayed that prayer, heaven is rejoicing. Jesus is excited to have you in His kingdom. Ask Him to show you someone strong in the faith to connect with so you can be encouraged and connected to some of His other children.

PART 2

I AM

FORGED IN FIRE EXCERPT:

*"Standing on the doorstep was the man who had
significantly influenced my teenage years. He led youth
camps across South Texas every summer and included
me in them. From when I was twelve until I turned
eighteen, he treated me as an apprentice and introduced
me to the prominent church leaders in Texas. Those
times were invaluable to my professional development.
He said, "I need somebody to help me understand my
church's hurting people. I need somebody to minister to
the people who suffer, somebody they can trust. You're
the right man for that role."*
*Sitting very still, I thought, "Dear God, he wants me.
Somebody wants me."*

D ave was beginning to rebuild his life when a man
who had been instrumental in his early development
came to his door. When that happened, it gave Dave
renewed hope and helped open the door to an old dream
that seemed impossible.

Traumatic events can overshadow everything in our
lives. We can lose sight of the fact that God has been
shaping and molding us for our entire lives so we can live
out His plan for us. As you reflect on your life, remember
to consider the good things you have learned, skills you
have developed, and people you have connected with
over the years. Some people have come into our lives
and modeled things for us that we would not have seen

if we had not crossed paths. Some of our life attitudes come from them.

Those role models can be very positive influences in our lives. Others along our paths, however, may have modeled how not to do things or live our lives. We can still value having them on our path to help us define what we don't want.

Scripture is filled with accounts of people who had trauma throughout their lives, yet, God used everything that happened to strengthen them and help them be victorious.

Take Moses, for example. He was marked for death as an infant, and when he was put into a basket and set afloat in the river, he was taken into the palace of the Pharoah to be raised in the royal household. Because he was raised in the royal household, he knew and understood the mind of the man he would need to convince to let God's people go.

As he became a man, he saw the injustices and the harsh disrespectful ways the Egyptians treated his people. That helped create a desire in him to work hard to serve God and free the Hebrews. It also led him to kill an Egyptian who was beating a Hebrew. When he discovered that some of the Hebrews had seen him do that, he understood that even his own people wouldn't understand that he was trying to help them. He was filled with guilt and fled into the wilderness. He was estranged from the Hebrews and the Egyptians.

At that point, he was set adrift from all he had known. He had no home, no identity, no future, and no purpose in his life. He left Egypt after 40 years of watching Pharoah and the leaders who surrounded him. He then lived in exile in Midian for 40 years as he worked as a shepherd and learned the ways of his Hebrew wife's family. As he shepherded the flocks in the desert, he learned how to survive in the wilderness and protect what had been entrusted to him.

Everything he experienced in his life contributed to helping him become a strong, powerful leader who served God and allowed Him to save His people. His past shaped him, gave him tools to build on, and inspired him to fulfill what God had planned for his final 40 years.

Did you notice something else about Moses? He survived it all. He had resilience. He faced whatever came next, reached down inside, and found the strength and resiliency to survive.

If you have survived trauma and are reading this today, you are also a person of strength and resilience. Acknowledge that fact and let it encourage you today. You may have hard healing work ahead of you, but you have inside you what you need to get through it all.

As you look back over your life, get clear about the parts of you that will be used for your future path. Make a gratitude list of the connections, skills, abilities, personality, and everything else that is part of your life. Remember to include your strength and resiliency that have helped you survive.

SCRIPTURE STUDY:
WHAT HAS GOD DONE?

Ephesians 2:10

Psalm 139:1-18

Matthew 6:25-32

Focus: *God's Handiwork*

> *"For we are God's masterpiece. He has created us anew in Christ Jesus, so we can do the good things he planned for us long ago."*

God creates. That is evident in every detail of the world. He could have spoken "universe," and he would have finished creating everything in the world in one holy second. Yet, His Word tells us He took six days. He painstakingly created everything so that it all came about in an orderly fashion.

Every part of creation has a purpose and is designed to perfection. Earth could not have supported human life if it had been even slightly closer to the sun or slightly farther away. He created us, and each of us is a beautiful reflection of Him placed in the world at the perfect time.

Scripture relates that God's Spirit hovered over the formless, void earth. Then God spoke, and step after step, He brought forth the world where we live. If He can do that from a void, He can do so much more in your life today because it is not void.

God created you and has shaped your life. In Psalm 139, you read that He knows you, that He thinks of you, and that He has plans for all your days. You are a masterpiece of His creation and needed for the good things He has planned for you.

Consider spending time building up your view of where you are today. Celebrate everything that gave you the strength that brought you through all the hard things to this point. Refuse to let trauma diminish you or who you are today. God is so much bigger than your trauma, and He still creates. Ask Him to show you what He is creating for you as you heal and recover from the effects of what you have been through.

HEARTWORK

After prayer and time in the presence of God, write out what He has shown you.

Discover

What has He revealed about the connections, skills, talents, and influences He has brought into your life over the years?

Define

What does each of those mean?

How have you been shaped and strengthened by each of them?

How can you benefit today by having those things in your life?

Defeat

What seems to be attempting to defeat the good things He has brought you? How can you reclaim what He has given you? Ask Him to show you the next steps He wants for you to take.

ONE VICTOR'S VOICE
IT'S DIFFERENT, BUT IT AIN'T OVER

Before the nurse began the procedure that day, she asked to see my arm bracelet. That was the new way I was identified. A number and my birthdate were the only remnants of who I had been before all this started. It seemed that is all I would ever be for the rest of my life. Just another victim, just another person for another procedure, and on the bad days, just another bother to anyone around me.

But this day, as I showed her the bracelet, a voice inside me asked, *"Do you see that date on the bracelet?"* I acknowledged that I did, and the voice quietly continued. *"I planned that."* I waited for a moment, then heard, *"Do you see the death date?"* Not sure what was coming next, I tentatively acknowledge I did not. Then I heard, *"You are still here, so, My plan is still in progress."*

That day, I stopped being a victim that was just a number and date. I spent time taking stock of everything that was an element and facet of me. I began to dust it off and fit all the pieces back together again. The first thing on my list was "overcomer." I had come through a tremendous, horrific thing. I had proven to myself that I could overcome everything keeping me from getting back to my life.

My life looks different now, but, knowing that God was with me through all the hard things gives me new courage and confidence that He has a great plan for me. I don't want to miss a minute of it!

PART 3

LOSS

FORGED IN FIRE EXCERPT:

"I felt responsible for those children's deaths and the village's destruction. It was the most horrible day of my life. This was a terrible irony; trying to be friendly, I had placed the women and children in grave jeopardy. And I, the Pied Piper of Thu Thua, was responsible for the enemy incinerating those children's corpses and eradicating the last vestiges of that village's existence. I didn't speak as we went back to the base. I also didn't cry or shed any tears.

Translated into English, Thu Thua means "lose, lose." It was a place where all involved did indeed lose. They lost innocent people, the way of life in that small village, and the future of what might have been for them all. I lost the vision that men can overcome evil simply by doing good."

In the last chapter, you were encouraged to identify and list elements of your life that have contributed to you being who you are. Hold tight to all you were shown as you begin the journey of healing the deep hurts inflicted by trauma.

Things have changed in your life because of what happened. Dave modeled transparency about what it was like for him. He had obvious scars and the courage to stand up in front of others and talk about his healing journey. You may also have suffered grave physical injuries that are obvious to all. Or, perhaps, your scars are all on the inside.

As this excerpt from his book reveals, Dave had some scars on the inside and outside. Often the inner pain is more difficult to heal because it isn't readily evident to people in your life.

Have you ever had a splinter lodged deep in your finger? Sometimes, you can't get a good enough grasp on it to extract it easily. If left in, however, it will begin to fester, bringing pain to an ever-increasing circle around it. When it becomes too painful to bear, most people will do whatever it takes to get it out. Once it is out, healing can begin.

When pain from trauma is inside you, it is like having a splinter in your heart. The longer it is left, the more it festers. Far too frequently, people who have experienced deep loss feel that it is not safe to tell other people about what happened. Time will heal this. No one else will understand. If I tell people about my part in this, everyone will hate me. Talking about it won't change anything, so why talk about it? These are all common untrue statements people hold as truth that keep them silent. That is when the splinter in the heart festers until it fills the entire body with dis-ease. People can't be at ease with God, other people, or even with themselves when deep pain is festering in their hearts.

Dave could not allow himself to cry over his loss. Some pain is so deep it can seem that if we allow ourselves to start crying, we will never stop.

When we take the shroud of darkness off of what happened, acknowledge what we feel, and define the loss, we can defeat its debilitating effect on our life.

God's refining fire will bring you through the pain and give you a new vision and purpose for your life. Talk to Him, be honest, and identify your greatest loss. Identify why it is so hard in your life now.

Consider letting someone else into your life to help you lift this burden. Scripture encourages us to "weep with those who weep." Ask God to bring a trustworthy person you can talk to into your life. You also have a Savior known as a "man of sorrows, acquainted with deepest grief" who "keeps track of all your sorrows, collects all your tears in a bottle, and records each one in His book." Spend time talking to Him about how much it hurts.

Cry, let yourself feel the feelings. There is an entire book in the Bible called Lamentations simply because God understands sadness. Letting the dammed-up pain from deep loss break loose will help wash away the anguish you are feeling. After all, even Jesus wept.

SCRIPTURE STUDY:

Jesus Raises Lazarus, Luke 11

Focus: *Jesus Wept*

Lazarus and his sisters, Mary and Martha, were some of Jesus' closest friends. They knew Him well, had witnessed His miracles, and followed close to Him.

Throughout this account, it is clear that:

Jesus knew all along that He would raise Lazarus from the dead.

He knew that many would come to believe because He would raise Lazarus.

He knew that death is not forever.

AND YET HE WEPT!

The Lord saw his friends' pain, and He cried. He was right there in the middle of all those people, and He cried. He sees our pain today. He cares about what you are going through, and He cries because of your pain.

When Mary said her brother wouldn't have died if Jesus had been there, He knew she believed He could have healed her brother. Yet, she thought He just hadn't done it for her.

Do you believe that Jesus loves you enough to heal your hurts?

He did great work through the deep loss in this family. He is still at work today. Spend time, define your loss, and talk to God about it all. Give God your loss; in exchange, He has a beautiful plan and purpose to give you.

HEARTWORK

After prayer and time in the presence of God, write out what He has shown you.

Discover

Make a list of all that you have lost. Be sure to let God show you things you may not have acknowledged before. Let God show you the sorrow and pain you are trying to hold inside; ask Him what He has to say to you about that.

Define

What does that loss mean to your life? Define how the loss of one thing may have triggered the loss of something else. Ask Jesus where He was during your loss; ask Him what He has to say to you about this.

Defeat

To heal from loss, it is healthy to grieve through the loss with someone who has compassion. Ask God for safe godly people in your life to go to so you can share your grief. Ask Him to bring someone who has overcome their grief to come into your life to be with you in your grief.

Ask Holy Spirit to draw near and comfort you.

ONE VICTOR'S VOICE
IT TURNS OUT REAL MEN DO CRY

I was always exhausted. No matter how much I slept, I woke up tired. My days were foggy at best and out of focus altogether at worst. I moved through everything I did with a sense that I wasn't really present in what was going on around me. When people asked, my standard reply was, "I'm fine. Doing great." The truth was I didn't know how I was because I was numb.

I couldn't let go of the shock of what happened. How could I? That was the moment my heart shattered, and I knew nothing would ever be the same again. Every time I remembered, my eyes would briefly fill with tears; but then, from somewhere inside, I would hear words echoing from my long-ago past, *"Suck it up, be a man. Do you want the other kids to laugh at you?"*

When my buddy asked me to go to a men's retreat with him, I really didn't want to go, but he wouldn't take no for an answer. Now, I'm glad he didn't. There was a difference in everything that happened that weekend.

They broke us into discussion groups, and one of the men in my group began to talk about how sad he was about what had happened in his life. He had tears running down his face. Because he was so honest, I felt safe with these guys. I physically felt something inside me break off, and I began to tell them what I was going through. I cried, then I cried some more. It seems weird to tell about, but all these big tough guys were there for me and helped me be able to open up.

As they prayed for me at the end, I was flooded with peace that I can't explain. Now I'm meeting weekly with one of the guys who has been through something similar. We are reading the Bible and praying, and every day is a little better than the one before.

PART 4

NEW ROBE

FORGED IN FIRE EXCERPT:

*"Beaching our boats on the grassy riverbank, we
flushed out the bunkers, captured some VC prisoners,
and began the body count. Seeing the bodies always
made me sick at heart. Several questions always
haunted me; "Did I kill that guy in the bunker? Did I
kill any of the dead?" We left the bodies on the blood-
stained ground and took our prisoners back to the base
in our boats.*
*The conflicting emotions of being involved in the intense
firefight were draining. I felt elated that I was still alive
and sick at the sight of the casualties.*

Did I kill that guy? During the firefight, Dave didn't
know for sure. He did have the gut-wrenching
knowledge that he had been part of the carnage left
behind in war. Combat in war-torn countries leaves
trauma in people's souls. It is a life-changing experience
that brings with it darkness into the heart of a person
and can leave shadows for years. Bringing death or
great harm to another person is contrary to how we are
created. God created life; death was not in His original
design for mankind.

Working to heal from war wounds from personal
combat is an important, in fact, a critical part of letting
the Holy Spirit bring healing to your soul. There are
many ways to seek help from trained counselors to deal
with the pain of your journey in combat. It is wise to

find help from someone trained in combat recovery if it is still a controlling factor in your life.

One of the residual feelings from combat is guilt. When you are in the military, you must follow the command of the officer in charge of you and the troops serving alongside you. You are not guilty when you engage in battle under officers' orders. You are part of facing a force that is trying to destroy and overrun other countries and people's lives. You know that intellectually, yet, how can you handle the persistent feeling of guilt?

Guilt is an element in everyone's life. Healthy guilt comes when we do something we know is wrong. The Word of God tells us that *"all have sinned and fall short of the glory of God."* Does this fact mean we should all walk through life robed in sackcloth? When we do something wrong, how long should we feel guilty? When does guilt do a perfect work in our soul, and when is it a sin?

When we do thoughtless, selfish, inconsiderate things, we feel guilty. When we lie, yield to the desires of our flesh in ways God never intended, slander, gossip, or intentionally hurt other people, guilt is a proper reaction.

Jesus sent the Holy Spirit to guide us. When we act against God's ways, we are guided to feel guilt. God loves His children far too much to let us get comfortable living outside the life He designed for us to live. When sin comes in, correction follows and brings a sense of guilt.

When we realize the price Christ Jesus paid so that our sins could be forgiven and we could reconcile with God, we have a very specific reaction. Godly sorrow floods our hearts. That sorrow produces repentance.

Repentance is admitting to God what we have done and expressing the deep sorrow we feel over what we did.

39

It also means turning away from what we have been doing and turning to Jesus, so we follow His ways. Repentance sets our minds and hearts back on God and keeps them from being focused on what happened.

Guilt is like a red light on the dashboard of a car. It alerts us to realize we are not aligned with the "factory settings" we had when we were born again.

Confession and repentance are the steps to reset us to our Manufacturer's settings of being forgiven, so we are in right relationship with God.

Like everything else he can come up with, the enemy of our souls wants to separate us from God, so he has perverted guilt. When we are feeling condemned, it is not God we are hearing.

When we robe ourselves in a sackcloth robe of guilt and shame, refuse to get honest with God, or grieve through what we have done, we achieve the enemy's purpose. We distance ourselves from God.

Inappropriate guilt comes when we feel responsible for something we have no power to control or any way to change. Inappropriate guilt leaves us covered in shame, questioning our value as a person. We change our "I did. . ." to "I am. . ." Instead of "I told a lie," we believe "I am a liar."

In combat, you must obey orders and do as you have been trained. It doesn't mean you won't feel sadness at the outcome. It is completely appropriate to feel that sadness. However, when you put on guilt, you allow it to keep you locked in the past darkness.

We are powerless to go back and change what happened in the past. When we stay focused on the past, we miss the life God has planned for us today. The irony is that war is usually fought for the cause of freedom, yet, it can leave brave, innocent soldiers locked behind life-stealing bars of inappropriate guilt.

When trauma from other situations comes into our life, it also can leave inappropriate feelings of guilt. When parents divorce, children frequently come to believe they caused it. When people are abused, they can infer that they were somehow deserving of or the cause of the abuse. If a child dies, a surviving sibling feels guilty because they weren't the one who died. Parents forced into working several jobs to keep a roof over their children's heads feel guilty if their child gets into trouble. When despair leads a loved one to commit suicide, inappropriate guilt leaves family and friends with the unanswerable question, "What else should I have done?" The list of types of guilt from trauma is long and very sad.

Whether you carry guilt or false guilt, your healing comes from the same solution.

Get honest with your heavenly Father, ask Jesus to send more of the Holy Spirit to help you see the truth, and confess any sin that separates you from His presence. Ask Him to speak to you about the whole matter. Bring all the detail into His Light so it can no longer hide in the shadows in your soul. Pour out your sorrow, so He knows what it is like for you. Then be quiet. Listen for what He has to say to you.

You are a God-created, Blood-bought, Holy Spirit-led child of God. When we judge ourselves as guilty of a sin so great it cannot be forgiven, we speak lies about His child, one of His most highly prized treasures.

No matter what you did, once you confess it with Godly sorrow and repent of it, only one adjective defines you about that matter. FORGIVEN.

His word in First John 1 says, *"If we confess our sins, He is faithful and just to forgive us our sins and to cleanse us from all unrighteousness."* When Jesus went to the cross, the work of salvation and the forgiveness of our sins was completed.

Some think, *"Jesus has forgiven me, so why do I need to confess and ask for forgiveness?"* Think about it like this. If a friend borrows a tool from you and thoughtlessly forgets to return it for a long time, you probably would have no problem forgiving them. We are all busy, and we sometimes forget. But when your friend comes to you and confesses his negligence, tells you he is sorry, then asks for forgiveness, he is showing you he cares about the relationship he has with you. We must always remember that God's heart desires to be our God and for us to choose to be his children so that He can live in a relationship with us.

The fact that Jesus paid the price for our sins is an amazing gift. When we know we have sin in our lives and don't bring it before Jesus, we disrespect and minimize what He has done for us.

When Jesus declared His earthly ministry, He said that His coming had fulfilled the prophecy found in Isaiah 61. That Scripture is His Ministry Statement as it tells what the Lord has anointed Him to do. Part of that mission is to *"Comfort all who mourn, to console those who mourn in Zion, to give them beauty for ashes, the oil of joy for mourning, and the garment of praise for the spirit of heaviness."*

There is no robe as heavy as a sackcloth robe of guilt. It weighs us down. It suppresses our joy. It keeps us from living our life. He wants to take that off of you and clothe you in a garment of praise. Wouldn't you rather wear that?

SCRIPTURE STUDY:
WHICH ROBE IS YOURS?

Romans 7:24 – 8:4; & 3:23; 6:23

Acts 22:19-21

2 Corinthians 7:10

Colossians 1:11-14

Ephesians 1:3-14, 4: 17-24

Hebrews 8:12

Focus: *Condemnation*

Our study of what Scripture says about guilt begins with a man who maliciously and intentionally went on a mission to end Christianity once and for all. There was no denying his guilt. Saul of Tarsus was a highly educated, privileged son of Jewish parents. He was clear about his mission in life. He was a zealous persecutor of Christians. He was good at what he did; in fact, he caused havoc in the church. He entered homes and dragged men and women off to prison. It appears that he was the one in charge as overseer at the stoning death of one of the most faithful, spirit-filled followers of Jesus, Stephen. Scriptures relate that Saul "approved the execution" and that the angry mob laid their "garments" at his feet.

Then he met Jesus. For those who have ever had the concept of an angry, vengeful God who is just waiting to catch us in the wrong, consider carefully what Jesus said to him. "Saul, Saul, why are you persecuting Me?"

There is no name-calling, judgment-declaring, shame-giving accusation. Just a simple, "Why?" He didn't ask the question because He wanted Saul to develop a defense. He didn't ask the question because He didn't know the answer. He asked the question so Saul could understand why he was doing what he was doing.

Having a blinding Light experience changed Saul immediately. His response to Jesus was, "Lord, what do You want me to do?"

Jesus came into his life and guided him down a path that led to a revelation about what was in his heart, and over time, to his healing. He then lived a life of being used in mighty ways to establish the Christian church.

When he was first mentioned, he went by Saul. That was his given Jewish name. He was a Roman citizen, so He also had a Latin name, Paul. As his healing continued, he became known as Paul, which fit the new person he had become.

The Scriptures above were penned by a man who recorded the Truth that Holy Spirit revealed to him about guilt, grace, mercy, and forgiveness as he learned about it himself. As he wrote to encourage churches, he included imagery of Believers taking off what they had worn and putting on what Jesus wanted them to wear.

He was speaking as one who knew to those who had also taken off their robe of guilt and shame when he said, "You have stripped off your old sinful nature and all its wicked deeds. Put on your new nature, and be renewed as you learn to know your Creator and become like him." Those are wise words for us all today.

Seek God diligently so He can heal your pain and restore your life. Ask Him which robe He wants you to wear.

HEARTWORK

After prayer and time in the presence of God, write out what He has shown you.

Discover

What guilt are you holding on to?

Ask Jesus to show you why you are clinging to it.

Is there any inappropriate guilt that you are now aware of?

Define

What purpose is your guilt serving?

Ask Jesus if what happened in your life is unforgivable.

Listen and believe what He has to say to you about what happened.

How is guilt keeping you bound to the past?

What is guilt keeping you from so your peace and joy can be restored?

Defeat

What is Holy Spirit saying to you about the guilt?

Ask Holy Spirit to come and purify your soul from all guilt and shame.

Ask what God wants to give you in exchange for you letting go of the guilt.

Be willing to accept what He has for you.

ONE VICTOR'S VOICE
CLINGING TO GUILT

"Batman" was a great guy. He never met a stranger, was always ready for a laugh, and drinks in the officer's club were always more fun when he was around. When we flew on missions together, I never wondered if he would carry his load. He was a solid guy.

I got orders to return to the US for reassignment and was packing when he came over and stuck out his hand. As we shook hands, he said, "I'm right behind you, buddy. I'll leave in four months, and I can't wait to get back to Linda and those kids."

We made plans to meet up when he returned, then said our goodbyes. I was glad our friendship would continue.

Two days after I left, he was shot down during a firefight and never made it home to see his wife and kids again. I was shocked when I heard about it; then I got mad at the enemy all over again. Then came the guilt.

Thoughts ran through my mind. *If I had been with him, I could have saved him. It should have been me; he had a four-month-old daughter he never got to meet. If he had to die, I should have been there with him and died, too.* On and on it went.

I climbed into the only source of comfort I knew, but even alcohol couldn't numb this guilt and the shame it brought into my soul. For years I felt responsible. During those years, my life was on a downward spiral. Then my circumstances forced me to get help.

One day my counselor sat looking at me quizzically for a long moment and then said, "So, let me see if I have this straight. Your good buddy died, and you have made choice after choice that has destroyed your life. Why is that?"

That was the falling domino question that triggered the beginning of my healing.

My guilt wasn't logical. Through my healing process, I discovered that it was a repeating pattern that went back to when I was a kid. Several times, my mom was in awful situations, my dad was deployed all the time, and I felt responsible for helping her. I couldn't, and it always left me feeling guilty.

My healing continued and ultimately led me to work through all the issues with God. It was with Him where I found peace. It was with Him that I discovered I didn't deserve the punishment I thought I deserved. It was where I got free and began to live.

I still think of Batman. Sometimes a memory of something funny he said will cross my mind, and a smile comes to my face. When I think of what all of us lost because we didn't have him around any longer than we did, I still shed tears.

I guess none of us will fully understand some of what life throws at us until we get to heaven, but at least now, I understand there are some things we can't control.

I'm grateful that I now know where to go to heal those hurts.

PART 5

NAME YOUR PAIN

FORGED IN FIRE EXCERPT

*"I was struck with a lightning bolt of soul-searing
pain when I looked into that mirror. I can tell you
that being burned is a shriveling pain that makes you
feel like you're being sucked into the air about you.
My soul seemed to shrivel, collapse on itself, and be
sucked into a black hole of despair. I was left with
an indescribable and terrifying emptiness. I was alone
in the way the souls in hell must feel. Jesus used the
psalmist's words when He cried, "My God, my God,
why hast thou forsaken me?"*

There is purpose in pain. When there is physical pain,
it functions to let us know there is something wrong
in some part of our body. When we have pain, we seek
the cause to be able to treat the source of the pain to
relieve our discomfort.

Physical pain is also a great teacher. We quickly learn that
touching something hot results in pain, so we use caution
the next time we are around anything hot. Since we don't
like to feel pain, we learn to avoid anything that will cause it.

The pain leaves visible evidence of the trauma
when you have physical trauma because of war, abuse,
accidents, or mistakes. There are trained physicians and
specialized treatments for the chronic physical pain that
can bring great physical relief.

In Dave's story, he suffered intense physical pain when his body was set on fire by a white phosphorus grenade. For days, he was in a fog of physical pain that was, at times, almost unbearable.

The excerpt above recounted an experience when the physical pain had lessened somewhat; then, he saw the visible evidence of his trauma. He suffered a new, intensely devastating pain. His soul was burning with pain. He couldn't wrap his mind around the fact that he was scarred beyond recognition; he felt emptied of his very life, felt separated from other people since he was now hideous, and his will was devoid of power as despair settled over him.

Our souls, made up of our mind, emotions, and will, can suffer intense pain from trauma. Soul wounds bring just as much pain as physical pain, yet, they don't leave visible evidence of the trauma. They are frequently difficult to describe. We know there is pain, yet, we can't put it into words that others can understand. When we have physical pain, we use words like burning, searing, aching, sharp, etc., to identify our feelings. Soul pain is not as easily described.

Pain in our soul is real and brings many valid emotions about the pain. When we express what we are feeling, we connect to others. The human journey is filled with pain and emotions that bind us to each other. Expressing our emotions is a powerful way to help others; it is also a way to be helped by someone else.

Pain in our soul is inflicted in many ways, and trauma can result in multiple layers of soul wounds. In Dave's example, the ones that come to light are humiliation, rejection, and injustice. He may have feared he would be abandoned and betrayed.

The pain was real. His soul was in deep pain. Soul wounds are the ones that bring pain to the very deepest level of our being since they shake our understanding of our identity and the foundation of our life. When soul pain is allowed to fester, it begins to paralyze lives. Dave showed great courage when he chose to seek God's purpose for his life. He could have withdrawn and let his soul wounds keep him from risking further rejection or ridicule.

To avoid anything that could cause pain, people will withdraw. Even when people find the courage to venture out, it dulls life's experiences. That sets up increased pain. The pain from what was is now compounded by never knowing what joy there might have been in those missed experiences.

Extreme soul pain can seem too big to explain to others. Just like physical trauma can cause soul pain; conversely, soul pain can cause physical pain when it isn't dealt with in healthy ways. Many medical studies link diseases of the body to unresolved soul pain. It is not unusual to experience physical pain that comes from soul trauma.

Symptoms in the body can be managed, but there is no medicine, surgery, or procedure to stop the soul pain so healing can begin. One source who understands and will bring you through the pain is always available to help. He will also show you the purpose of the pain. He didn't cause the trauma, but He won't waste a bit of the pain it has caused you to bring you closer to Him.

No matter what trauma you suffered, He understands the pain you are going through. He has been through it, too.

Consider Jesus' last days on earth. During his ministry, he miraculously healed, delivered, restored, and encourage people everywhere He went. He brought the good news that God still wanted to live in a relationship with people if they would repent and turn to God. He had throngs of followers who loved and celebrated Him. Then came that fateful last week.

He asked God to change what was about to happen, but He knew what He would have to do. His last days on earth, when he was fulfilling His mission, don't reflect the amazing miracle God was doing through Him. A close friend betrayed him, and his followers scattered and denied Him. He was whipped with thorns and brambles, then by whips with spiked tips until his skin was falling off His body; people spit on Him, made fun of Him, and then He was nailed on a cross, stripped naked, and hung up so the people could shame Him.

He knows pain. He has felt soul wounds of betrayal, humiliation, rejection, abandonment, and injustice. He will never minimize your pain and what you are feeling because of it.

When He created each of us, God created us in His image. Scripture reveals many emotions that God feels. He is never governed by emotions the way we can be, but He has emotions.

The Father experienced deep pain because of His deep love for us. He was not removed from Jesus' journey to the cross; He was there and experienced the pain of seeing His son reap the wages of our sins to become our sacrifice and atonement. He didn't forsake Jesus; however, when all the sin was laid on Jesus, He had to turn away from the sin. His deepest pain of all eternity may have been when His son called out, "Abba, why have you forsaken me?"

He knows and understands the pain you are feeling. He hasn't forsaken you, either. He wants to walk through your pain with you. He wants to reveal the purpose that can come from this deep soul wound. He wants to take the pain and leave you with a purpose that can shape and form a more abundant life than you have ever imagined.

SCRIPTURE STUDY:
WHERE IS GOD?

Hebrews 12:1-3   Revelation 21:3-4

Psalm 69:29-30   Matthew 26:53-54

Focus: *Consider Jesus*

Jesus chose the cross because of the joy that was set before Him. Having a relationship with each of us is His joy. Sometimes, a relationship with Him deepens when we walk onto a pathway to Him through a doorway called pain. Pain in our body pushes us to seek physical help. Pain in our soul pushes us to seek Him.

Most people hurry to a doctor to find a way to lessen their physical pain in a temporal body that will one day cease. Why do we carry wounds in our eternal souls for years without seeking help from Jesus? When we seek Him, we will discover far more about His character and nature than we may have ever known if we hadn't had the pain. The more we know of Him, the more we want to be with Him. The closer we draw to Him, the more we discover who we are truly meant to be. It gives purpose to our greatest pain.

God works through His people to bring about His plan on earth. He never wanted any of us to suffer pain. However, the fallen world we live in brings many hurtful situations into our lives, often leaving us feeling pain so deep that it seems insurmountable.

He uses people who have survived and healed from great pain to share their experiences with others who need to hear how He helped heal them. He knows the ones that will need to hear your story of victory. You may be able to reach someone who is giving up. He is encouraging you today to choose to draw close to Him so that He can heal your pain and you can reach others. Soul pain has already stolen too much from you; refuse to let it steal your victory.

HEARTWORK

After prayer and time in the presence of God, write out what He has shown you.

Discover

What has He revealed about the pain in your soul?

Has He revealed any physical pain that is coming from the soul pain you are carrying?

Do you now see the fear you have had about telling others about the pain in your soul?

Ask Jesus what He wants to say to you about any physical or soul pain you are carrying.

Define

What effect does your pain have on your life?

Are interactions with others limited?

Does it keep you safe from painful situations?

How have you learned to try to protect yourself from further pain?

Ask Jesus if He will draw close to you to protect and guide you.

Defeat

Ask Holy Spirit to come and heal you of all pain.

Seek all that God wants to show you, or say to you about the pain.

Ask for a vision of what your life will be like when the pain is healed.

Let Holy Spirit highlight Scriptures that promise and assure you that God heals.

Trust God to heal you.

ONE VICTOR'S VOICE
CHANGE OF FACE

I can't remember many details about the day I first felt the pain. But I have never forgotten the pain. I remember all the adults around me that day had red faces and loud voices. They were all yelling at once, and it kept getting louder. Then I felt the searing pain in my stomach. The pain was so intense that I started to cry and ran into my room.

When the front door finally slammed, and silence returned, it became apparent that I was missing. My mother came into my room and sat beside me. She smoothed my hair back from my face with trembling hands. I remember thinking that my insides were trembling, just like her hands.

I battled episodes of life-pausing pain for the next twenty-four years. Each time a difficult, uncomfortable, or threatening situation came up for me, it was averted because I took to my bed wracked with pain. Doctor after doctor came back with the same report. There was no cause for the pain.

One year for my birthday, my mom gave me a "memory book" that captured my life in pictures from my past. As I flipped through the book, I noticed a marked difference in my appearance. At first, I looked so happy. I was the one with the biggest grin and brightest eyes until the pain started. In the rest of the pictures, any smile I put forth never really reached up to my eyes.

Those pictures triggered something down in my soul, and I knew the truth of what had been happening. Sitting there with the pictures, one tear slid down my face. Then my stomach ache came to take my mind off what had happened. My body wouldn't let me feel what was in my soul.

I cried out to God that night. Surely, He didn't intend my life to be dominated by this pain and the isolation it caused me. I begged for help. He flooded me with peace, and even though I had no idea how, I knew this was going to end. I was going to get help. I thought I would wake up the next day completely healed.

Instead, He sent a gentle minister into my life at just the right time. She helped me discover the root of my pain. It wasn't my stomach that was the problem. The stomach became my defense. When anger in the people around me became uncontrolled rage, it hurt down in my soul. But when my stomach hurt, I focused on that pain, not the pain in my soul.

I've learned to pray through all of the past. Holy Spirit has been so powerful in showing all that I needed to know to be able to let the Lord heal the hurts in my soul. When I sense an unpleasantness in my family, now I ask Jesus to help me. I've learned to set boundaries. I've learned to speak up with clarity and truth. I've learned that I am loved and worthy, and it's not okay for others to use their rage to hurt me.

My life is pain-free now. Sometimes when I am out in the world, even strangers will look at me and tell me I have a beautiful smile. I always tell them I got it from my Father.

PART 6

ANGER

FORGED IN FIRE EXCERPT:

*"She started talking about getting a job to earn extra
income to contribute to our savings. I felt extremely
threatened by the idea of her going out in the world
daily. She would undoubtedly be around men who were
far more attractive than me. One day, the discussion
blew up and became a quarrel. I drew out my usual
weapon to get my way and loudly said, "I don't blame
you; I couldn't love me either." She didn't respond, and
her silence spoke volumes to me.*

*That was it! I grabbed my coat, stormed out of the
house, and jumped into the old truck we used as a
second vehicle. My driving reflected my anger as I flew
down the driveway and took off down the road."*

Anger is an extremely complex issue. Holy Spirit's
involvement is a must if lasting anger in our lives is
to be truly understood and its effects heal. Anger itself
is a basic component of our creation. When there is
danger, anger triggers the flight or fight response. We are
created to be survivors so we can thrive in the lives God
designed for us. Anger caused by a threat to God or His
design for people's lives is not a sin.

In fact, Scripture found in Ephesians 4 instructs us to
"Be angry, and do not sin; do not let the sun go down
on your wrath." It doesn't say that being angry is a sin.
However, like so many other things in the broken world
around us, anger has been perverted. Anger has become

an effective divisive tool to bring hostility which has fractured our culture on any topic you can name.

Anger as a tool is also the primary wedge driver in marriages today. A great question to ask is, "What are people so angry about?" Surprisingly some people who are angry most of the time can't truly answer that question. Another question to ask is, "Who are people so angry with?" Oddly enough, the outburst of anger is rarely directed toward the source of their anger.

The two most important questions to address are:

1. What is the right response to anger?

2. What is the real issue hiding behind lasting, unexplainable anger?

The right response to anger will never come from a place of self-righteousness. It is common when the topic of anger comes up for someone to say, well, Jesus had righteous anger and turned over the tables in the temple.

Indeed, He was angered because the court of the Gentiles that should have been reserved for people not of the Jewish faith to have a place to come, pray, and seek God was filled up with Jewish money changers taking dishonest money from the Temple. Not only were these men defying the instruction of the right use of God's temple, but they were also setting a terrible example of what being a child of God meant. He was right to turn over their tables. He had the right purpose and focus on why He was angry.

He did not **react to** what he saw in a fit of rage. Scripture tells us, *"When He had made a whip of cords, He drove them all out of the temple, with the sheep and the oxen, and poured out the changers' money and overturned the tables.* He **responded to** injustice with thought and prayer before

He took action. Throughout His earthly ministry, He said He only did what His Father told Him to do. After prayer, He took time to make a whip to drive the money changers out of the space designated for prayer so He could drive home his point.

Mark's gospel recounted a time when He was also angry with the Pharisees on a Sabbath. A man with a withered hand had come for healing, and the Pharisees thought the Sabbath was more important than healing the man in pain. *"And when He had looked around at them with anger, being grieved by the hardness of their hearts, He said to the man, "Stretch out your hand."*

Injustice and inconsiderate attitudes toward others, particularly in the name of religion, trigger anger. The anger comes because He is grieved when we aren't in unity with Him and others. Jesus is always compassionate and passionate about having a relationship with all of God's children.

The enemy of our souls wants us to take up offenses that come from others and direct our anger at them because they have wronged us. Jesus wants us to live in unity with each other and instructs us that if someone sins against us, we should go and discuss the issue. Discuss means being open and honest and willing to listen to the other person.

Usually, when we follow that instruction, it results in a closer relationship.

Anger is often classified as a secondary or a mask emotion since it covers up the real emotional issue. It appears to come from a position of strength which is more comfortable than letting others know we are feeling loss, sadness, or pain. For unexplainable reasons, those feelings can be perceived as weak. Actually, however, being able to be vulnerable enough to share the truth of our emotions takes a very strong person.

When we exhibit anger, it keeps people at a distance. That seems safer than being vulnerable about our loss, sadness, or pain. The problem with using anger to keep people away is that we are hurting other people and ultimately weakening our relationship.

In Dave's excerpt, he exposes the fact that he thinks if Brenda got a job, she would meet someone else and leave him. His irrational fear was that the real reason she wanted a job was so she could meet someone else. He used his anger to manipulate her to stay with him. In a deeper part of his soul, he may have thought he would use his anger to be the reason she left him. That, to him, on that deep inner level, would be easier than having her choose to leave him because she could not love him anymore.

When you feel anger caused today, it may be normal, and if responded to correctly, it may be harmless. The anger you hold on to for longer than today, however, may be rooted in bitterness and unforgiveness. When anger is rooted there, the enemy of your soul uses it to keep you separated from other people and distanced from God.

If you have waves of repeating, relentless anger dominating your life, there may be a wound in your soul in need of healing. Spend time with the Lord in prayer and seeking so you can understand why you are angry.

If you struggle to draw close to God, examine your heart to see if you are angry with Him. Do you blame Him for what happened, or perhaps even believe that he caused the trauma? He loves you enough to work through that with you. You can tell Him what you are feeling. You can ask Him questions.

One of the most frequently asked questions from people recovering from trauma is, "God, where were you when I was going through this?" If you have a relationship with Him as your Savior, He will answer that question for you. Biblical counselors can help you with this so you can move through the anger and into the answers He has for you.

When situations prompt anger, it is important to respond to the anger with the right purpose and the right focus. If we don't have that, we will **react** rather than **respond**. A reaction in the heat of the situation may cause more harm than good. It will rarely be with the right purpose or focus. Those uses of anger are destructive.

An old story has been told so long that its authorship is lost, but it is a wonderful illustration of what an inappropriate response to anger does in relationships.

> There once was a little boy who had a bad temper. His father gave him a bag of nails and told him that every time he lost his temper, he must hammer a nail into the back of the fence.
>
> The boy had driven 37 nails into the fence on the first day. Over the next few weeks, as he learned to control his anger, the number of nails hammered daily gradually dwindled. He discovered it was easier to hold his temper than to drive those nails.
>
> Finally, the day came when the boy didn't lose his temper at all. He told his father about it, and the father suggested that the boy now pull out one nail for each day that he was able to hold his temper. The days passed, and the young boy finally told his father that all the nails were gone.

The father led his son by the hand to the fence. "You have done well, my son, but look at the holes in the fence. The fence will never be the same. When you say things in anger, they leave a scar. If you put a knife in a man and draw it out, it won't matter how many times you say I'm sorry; the wound is still there."

The little boy then understood how powerful his words were. He looked up at his father and said, "I hope you can forgive me, father, for the holes I put in you."

"Of course, I can," said the father.

In His sermon on the mount, Jesus taught, *"You have heard that our ancestors were told, 'You must not murder. If you commit murder, you are subject to judgment.' But I say, if you are even angry with someone, you are subject to judgment! If you call someone an idiot, you are in danger of being brought before the court. And if you curse someone, you are in danger of the fires of hell."*

He set the benchmark for how to control our anger when it comes. All Christians are grateful that there is fresh mercy every day and that forgiveness is always given when we repent and turn back to Him. Like the little boy in the story, The Lord wants us to always be mindful of the lasting effects inappropriate responses to anger have on people who share our lives.

SCRIPTURE STUDY:
MATTHEW 5:21-23

Ephesians 4: 26-32   Proverbs 19:11

James 3:5-9;   Proverbs 15:4

Psalms 141:3   Proverbs 21:23

How Jesus handled anger:

Matthew 21:12-13, John 2:14-16, Mark 3:1-5

Focus: The Danger of Anger

Anger is not bad. It is inevitable and normal. When managed properly, it is a force that can help bring about needed change and often stir others to participate in the change. Mismanaged anger disconnects us from God, relationships, community, and sometimes from fellowship with other believers.

There are many layers of emotions around traumatic experiences. What you feel is never bad, but recognizing the root source of your anger will help you heal the past so you can thrive in your present life. Sadly, mismanaged anger can prevent people from having the very thing that was taken away from them by trauma.

Trauma upsets our "normal" and sets us adrift with the feeling that we can't ever return. When injustice, loss, and pain are covered up by the use of anger as a weapon, people are self-sabotaging the opportunity to gain back what was lost. Rather than letting the consuming fire of Holy Spirit come into our souls to heal the pain, loss, and injustice, anger uses the tongue to set our whole life on fire and burn down our relationships. Psalm 37 tells us, *Stop being angry! Turn from your rage! Do not lose your temper— it only leads to harm.* Rage harms everyone in a situation. This Scripture study contains insightful verses about the effects of our words. Pray for understanding and help as you read through those verses.

Perhaps, you have "scorched" relationships and opportunities, pray for wisdom from above to know how to restore and bring life back to what God has intended for you. The benefits of being a child of God are great and bless every area of our lives. They are listed in the 103rd Psalms. They reassure us that, Our Father *"redeems your life from destruction, crowns you with lovingkindness and tender mercies, satisfies your mouth with good things, so your youth is renewed like the eagle's."*

Give Him your anger, and He will fulfill this benefit for you.

HEARTWORK

After prayer and time in the presence of God, write out what He has shown you.

Discover

What are the things you are angry about?

Who are you angry with?

How long have you been angry?

Ask to see if your anger is allowing you to hide from deeper, uncomfortable feelings.

List all that you are shown.

Define

What is the root of everything on your list?

Have any of those root causes brought more situations that have made you angry?

How does your anger affect your relationships with other people?

With God? With yourself?

Have you caused relationship damage you want to repair? Ask Jesus to show you how to do that.

What do you think about yourself when you explode in anger?

Ask Jesus what He wants to say to you about your anger.

Ask Him to help you learn to respond rather than react when unpleasant things happen.

Defeat

What has Holy Spirit shown you through this work?

Are you willing to not only listen but to carry through with what you have been shown?

If Holy Spirit prompted you to make amends to someone, are you willing?

If your anger is keeping you from acknowledging deeper feelings, ask Holy Spirit to come and help you heal in those areas.

ONE VICTOR'S VOICE
WEAPON OF DESTRUCTION

Zack is the only man I ever loved. It sounds sappy, but the minute I met him, the world around me stood still. My heart was filled with a tender loving feeling when he turned and looked at me.

For the three years we dated, we had amazing, fun adventures. Our wedding was beautiful. His vows to me were wonderful and filled my heart with the promise that our marriage would be perfect. We were married for two great years before he deployed. We occasionally had little "spats," but we always got the issue resolved quickly. We never had any big problems.

I felt sick when he got orders to be deployed for twelve months. I did not want him to go at all, but that seemed far too long. We stayed in touch during that time, but his communication got shorter, and he shared less about what his life was like. I knew it was hard over there, and I tried to let him know I still loved him.

The day he returned was the happiest day ever. It was finally over, and now we could return to our lives and the plans we had made.

At first, it seemed like nothing had changed, but then it became apparent that he was struggling. He had nightmares and times when he didn't seem to hear or even see me. Then he started turning on me.

It seemed like I couldn't do anything right. The simplest thing I said would set him off on an angry explosion that made me want to run away. His words felt like an attack. The next thing I did would send him into dark silence, and he wouldn't even acknowledge me for days.

I demanded we get help. He said we didn't need any help. At those times, he would promise to act better toward me, and he would for a few days. Then the pattern would start up again.

One Sunday night, I dreamed I was raising a garden. The plants were wilting from lack of water, then some clouds came up, and I was glad because I thought it was rain. But the clouds turned orange, and big drops came from the clouds onto my plants. I realized it was poison and that this would kill off what I was growing. I woke up sweating because it seemed so real, and I was so afraid.

That morning, I packed my things, moved to my mom's, and found a divorce lawyer. I refused to stay in a marriage and watch as drop after drop of anger killed what I had thought we were growing.

That was ten years ago. Thankfully, people around us offered us help, and Zack was finally ready to accept it. When he could get honest about everything bottled up inside, I understood why it had been so hard. I shared his sadness over what had happened, and now I understood his pain and outrage. He finally let me in to share his life. I have been with him every step of his healing; each step has shown me what a truly brave person he is.

We have a 5-year-old son and a baby girl who bless our lives. We would never have had them if we hadn't worked this out. I thought we were really close before, but now we have grown closer than I even imagined people could be.

PART 7

BREAK IT UP

FORGED IN FIRE EXCERPT:

"Unfortunately, one area where I needed a great deal of growth and improvement was how I responded to Brenda. The unconditional love she showed me in so many different ways was still unbelievable. When there is no self-love for the person you have become, it is hard to believe that someone else can love you. One look in the mirror reminded me of the disfigured person, who was now her husband. I couldn't look past the man in the mirror and see that I was created in the image of God; therefore, I couldn't believe that she could either. Being able to accept unconditional, undeserved love was an essential step on the road to preparing to share the gospel. When I let go of the limitation I thought my scars had placed on my life, the possibilities of how God might use me to reach others flooded my soul."

Trauma brought an unsolicited, invisible gift to Dave. Because the physical effects were evident in his body, he received immediate medical attention, and healing began. Those around him readily saw what had happened to him physically and reacted with compassion and encouragement.

The unseen gift was a lie lodged deep in his soul that gave birth to a false label and untrue limitations. From the image in the mirror, he heard the lie, *"You are not the man you once were; you are too disfigured."* His broken heart formed the label *disfigured freak*. His soul lost his confidence, and his will responded to the self-imposed limitation, *unlovable*.

The image in the mirror was so convincing and shouted its false truth so loudly that Dave couldn't hear the Truth of his Father. Holy Spirit reminded him," *Can anything ever separate you from Christ's love? Does it mean He no longer loves you if you have trouble or calamity, are persecuted, hungry, destitute, in danger, or are threatened with death? No, despite all these things, overwhelming victory is yours through Christ, who loves you.* However, the vile father of lies always tries to drown out Our Father.

These wounds are not evident to the people around us. They often aren't even identified by those who have gone through trauma. They are like a computer's background system; they run continually and take little or no input from the user. Until they are identified, they work behind the scenes to build up strongholds that take over a soul. The longer they are left in place, the more soul territory they take over. The consuming fire of Holy Spirit wants to come in and take back that territory; it belongs to God.

Here is how strongholds work. First, trauma takes place. When that happens, the person forms a belief about what happened. A negative incident will result in a false belief being formed. It is a lie about themselves, other people or classifications of people, or God. Because of the pain caused by the trauma, a person thinks they are in charge of protecting themselves and will set up a defense. That defense will then come into play when they later interact with other people. If there is a strong defense in place, it will elicit a negative response from other people.

That negative response then causes another negative event, strengthening the appearance that their belief based on a lie is true. The cycle is endlessly repeated and grows stronger until the healing of the original hurt happens.

Here is the anatomy of Dave's stronghold. He was badly burned and scarred. He formed the belief that he was completely unlovable. His defense was to lash out in anger anytime he sensed that Brenda was going to leave him. His defense was harsh and hurtful to Brenda. She did love him and wasn't wanting to leave, but when Dave was angry with her, she withdrew. When she withdrew, it set up another negative event, proved that the lie he believed was true, and made him more defensive than ever. Each time the pattern repeated, the behavior, the false belief, and the unwarranted defense grew stronger.

Until the root cause of the soul wound is healed, it is like going to the gym daily and working on the bicep muscles. The more you repeat the exercise, the bigger and stronger the bicep becomes. The more spiritual strongholds are repeated, the bigger and stronger the lie becomes, the greater the defense grows, and the further away we push others. Brenda and Dave allowed God to reveal what was going on so they could overcome it.

Because of the nature of soul wounds, they are not easy to understand. If you have a repeating pattern of behavior, however, you may have something in your soul that needs attention because it has set up a destructive pattern in your life. God is our source of wisdom about any of our struggles. His word instructs us, *"If you need wisdom, ask our generous God, and he will give it to you. He will not rebuke you for asking."* In His wisdom, He also gave us Scripture to help us identify and define what a stronghold is. The Scripture study in this chapter will be an in-depth look at that.

One of Christians' foundational Scriptures is Jesus' instruction about being His follower. He said to His disciples, *"If any of you wants to be my follower, you must give up your own way, take up your cross, and follow me. If you try to hang on to your life, you will lose it. But if you give up your life for my sake, you will save it."*

This has many applications in our life; however, if you apply it to a life with strongholds, it has a clear and significant meaning. *Your own way* is built on the old lies, labels, and limitations embedded in your soul that keep us from becoming the person He created us to be. We created a way of life designed to protect ourselves from being hurt again. Being willing to open up to God to discover the root of the wound and let Him heal it is the first step.

Reaching for Him helps us stop holding on to the life trauma has formed. If we hang on to that life, we will lose the abundant life of joy He has planned for us.

SCRIPTURE STUDY:
WHAT IS A STRONGHOLD?

2 Corinthians 10:3-6

"We are human, but we don't wage war as humans do. We use God's mighty weapons, not worldly weapons, to knock down the strongholds of human reasoning and to destroy false arguments. We destroy every proud obstacle that keeps people from knowing God. We capture their rebellious thoughts and teach them to obey Christ."

Focus: Break The Cycle of Bondage

Strongholds keep us bound in isolation to the events of the past. Trauma carries with it a strong impact. But He that is in us is greater than trauma's impact. He has a plan for every life and wants to come in to keep us moving forward in our life. There is a process to break free from that bondage. No one can change the past or stop the past trauma from happening. It happened.

We can change what happens now by deciding to let the Lord come in and heal those hurts.

Continuing toward freedom requires the knowledge that you are in a battle. Everything that happened to you during trauma is being used in the battle for control of your soul. God created every person with a specific plan and a unique purpose. There is an enemy who wants to see you distracted, defeated, and destined to live with the labels and limitations trauma seems to have placed in your path.

Sidelining you negatively impacts your influence on God's kingdom. Fighting for your freedom is a powerful way to fight for the freedom of your family, friends, and those around you. The Lord needs you as an integral part of His kingdom.

Remember, your soul is your mind, emotions, and will. The primary battle happens in your mind. The good thing is that each one of us is in control of our minds. The devil can't control it, and God doesn't control it because He wants us to have the freedom of choice. However, it may not seem like you are in control right now.

Identifying the source of a thought is critical to healing. Dave looked in a mirror and believed he wasn't the man he once was, yet that wasn't true. We are created in God's image. Most of us are wrinkled, red, or even purple at birth with blue hands and feet. It's hard to see the image of God at that point.

If you have ever been present at the moment of birth, though, you know the spiritual presence of God is unmistakable. The outer physical body never limits the person He created us to be. That body is going to end one day. The person He created never will. Let's begin the work to break that person out of bondage.

Freedom Steps ~ to be done over several sessions. Write your answers so you can refer back to your responses. As you read the steps, think of them in light of the Focus Scripture. You are looking for strongholds of human reasoning, false arguments about God, and proud obstacles keeping you from His presence.

1. **List your trauma.**

   What was the event, or perhaps several events, that brought great pain, shock, anguish, or suffering into your soul?

   Ask Jesus to show you the first time you had trauma like this.

2. **Look for the strongholds of human reasoning and false arguments.**

   Write out what you came to believe because of the trauma.

   What did you believe about what caused it? What did you believe about the other people involved in it?

   What did you believe about yourself? What did you believe about God?

3. **List the generalized belief you came to hold as a primary belief.**

   Here is an example: a victim of childhood abuse believes the attacker was a bad person and should not have taken advantage of his vulnerability. They then generalize the belief, "All men are bad, and anytime I am vulnerable, they will attack me."

4. **Look for every proud obstacle that keeps you from others and from God.**

   For each belief, write down the ways you learned to defend yourself to keep it from happening again. i.e., The person in the example from step three would never allow themselves to be vulnerable around any man.

5. **Let God Be Your Protector**

   Read the Word to see what it teaches about God as our Protector.

   Ask Jesus if He will defend you.

   If you believe that Protector is His role, confess that you have believed that you have to protect yourself.

   Talk to Him, asking forgiveness for your protectionism, and grace to let go and let Him be involved in your life.

6. **List all you have come to believe about God because of your experience.**

7. **Identify any people that negatively responded to your defense strategies and set up more trauma in your life.**

8. **Take this work before the Lord. Prayerfully involve Holy Spirit to reveal all that is not of the Lord so it can be consumed and your heart will be purified.**

9. **For every thought that is a lie hurting your life, search for Scripture or a word from God to replace it.**

   You can't stop thinking a thought.

   You must replace it with the Truth.

10. **Capture your rebellious thoughts and teach them to obey Christ.**

    Activate your will.

    Memorize and believe the Word of Truth. When an old lie comes into your thoughts, rebuke it and speak the Truth God has shown you.

"Whenever someone turns to the Lord,
the veil is taken away.
For the Lord is the Spirit, and wherever the Spirit of
the Lord is, there is freedom.
All of us who have had that veil removed can see and
reflect the glory of the Lord.
And the Lord—who is the Spirit makes us more
and more like him as we are changed into his glorious
image.
2 Corinthians 3:16-18

He is with you; freedom is being offered to you. Will you accept His gift?

HEARTWORK

This is a "wrap up" exercise to the Freedom Steps. After prayer and time in the presence of God, once the steps are finished, spend time with Him for an overview, and new insights.

Discover

What has He revealed as the original trauma that caused your soul pain?

Where was Jesus during this? What has He revealed about what happened?

What are the lies you believed about yourself, God, and other people or types of people?

How have you tried to protect yourself from being hurt again?

What responses have you gotten from others because of the defenses you have in place?

Define

How long have you seen this stronghold pattern in your life?

When was the last time you realized that you were back in the same old pattern?

Identify the defenses you have which have gotten stronger over time.

Acknowledge the pain and loss you have in your life because of the strongholds.

Defeat

Ask Jesus if He will come into this stronghold cycle and allow you to let Him become your protector.

Ask Holy Spirit to address each of the lies you have been believing; ask for Truth that will replace those lies.

Memorize specific Scripture that addresses your situation.

To conquer this, choose to focus on the Truth of what you have been told, Trust Jesus to protect you, and continually ask Holy Spirit to heal your hurts and to give you courage.

ONE VICTOR'S VOICE
STRONG AND FREE

My dad was gone most of the time when I was a kid. When he was there, he drank heavily; the more he drank, the angrier he got. Since I thought I was the source of his anger, I tried to stay quiet and out of his way. I rarely made it through a day without him slapping me and calling me stupid or lazy. He finally left when I was in junior high. At first, I was glad he was gone. Then I saw how hard my mom had to work to feed us, and I felt like it was my fault my dad left, so I felt ashamed.

For the rest of my years growing up, I focused on proving to my dad that he was wrong. I studied hard and got a scholarship to college. I graduated in three, not four years, and started climbing the ladder. Anywhere I lived was a no-alcohol zone because it was associated with him.

When I got married, it was for life. We were married for twelve years and had three kids before I realized I had killed the relationship.

There was no room in my life for anything except performance. I couldn't accept "stupidity" into my world for myself or my family. Excellence, good performance, and worthy work were my only interests.

When my wife took my kids and left, I was devastated and lived in a fog of confusion. I had done everything right. I made money, showered gifts, and acted the way a devoted husband and father should act. On my knees in the middle of the darkest night I had ever gone through, I screamed out my complaint to God. "Why did you let this happen? I'm not stupid. I did everything right!"

His answer that night showed me what had claimed my soul and kept me locked in bondage for my entire life. *What you did was not wrong. But where was your heart?* That was said with so much tenderness that I started to cry. I knew the answer.

My heart was in the past. It was focused on proving I was worthy to a broken man who never broke out of his past to even notice me. With the grace and mercy of God and my wife, we went to counseling to work on those soul wounds.

I'm not chained to the past any longer, and our future together looks amazing. When I come before God, I ask Him to show me the wounds I have inflicted on my children. I want to help them heal the lies before they limit their lives. Thanks to a Father who has always known me and loved me, even when I didn't know Him, I'm learning how to love my kids and my wife.

PART 8

FORGIVENESS

FORGED IN FIRE EXCERPT:

"God did not create me as a scarred, weak man who only represented fox-hole faith.
How could my best friend, shepherd, and mentor see me that way?
The pain I felt at this seeming betrayal was intense. I pushed my coffee cup away, shoved my chair back so suddenly it tipped back, coming to rest at a forty-five-degree angle against the wall behind me, and then forcefully, I rushed out of his house."

The situation in this excerpt that caused the pain for Dave came out of nowhere. When this happened, he was relaxed, enjoying a cup of coffee with a close mentor and friend. His friend said his ministry would end when the Vietnam war ended. The anger behind Dave's actions hid the pain of being betrayed by someone so close. He left, but the pain and anger went with him, and the words, *"How could he?"* echoed in his soul.

A form of that question frequently echoes in the souls of people who have unhealed wounds. That unanswerable question locks us in the repeating strongholds discussed in the last chapter. It is often the question that holds us bound to the past because we struggle to forgive someone since it is inconceivable that they did such a hurtful thing.

Scriptures are filled with verses that command us to forgive. Other verses encourage us to forgive so we can be forgiven. Still others teach us to forgive because we have been forgiven. All of them are there in His Word because God is serious about forgiveness.

If we can begin to understand "how could he," we can begin to consider forgiving. Living in relationships with others helps us see that no one is perfect, we all make mistakes, and hurtful things sometimes happen because someone is thoughtless or inattentive.

Jesus teaches us to go to the person who has hurt us so the situation can be understood, forgiveness can be granted, and peace can be restored.

When we are willing to follow this instruction, we may find there was a misunderstanding of all the actions involved. It may be an opportunity to gain respect and more understanding with the other person.

Sometimes, the situation doesn't resolve peacefully, yet, we can grow from the experience of speaking up about our feelings. We are only responsible for taking the action of going to the other person with an attitude that encourages resolution; never are we told to go in anger and judgment. *"God has given us this task of reconciling people to Him."* We grow in our ability to do that when we go and offer to reconcile our relationships. Coming together to discuss a problem is a way to mature in our walk with Christ and other people.

A division between people sets in when we are hurt and harden our hearts toward the other person. We look at how we were wronged by them and build a case against the one who hurt us. We are in a position of a prosecuting attorney building the case, we are also the jury that decides if the proof is valid, and then we are the judge that declares "Guilty" over the other person.

If we continue to hold it against them in our hearts, we condemn them because of their sin.

This process takes our attention and our energy and keeps us from moving forward in our lives. The wrong is repeatedly replayed in our minds with increasing frequency. It is like watching an old rerun on television so often that it stays fresh in our minds as if it happened only minutes ago rather than years ago.

There are levels of hurt, and the graver, deeper, and more horrendous the trauma, the harder it is to forgive. When someone has entered into sin and hurt you with devastating pain, there is nothing wrong with speaking up and saying that it was a sin, it was devastating, and it was wrong of them to do that. It is never something we should keep secret or feel shame over. Forgiveness in these instances may require the process of working it out with God, and possibly through counseling.

We are created in God's image, and He hates sin. Proverbs 6 tells us, *There are six things the LORD hates — no, seven things he detests: haughty eyes, a lying tongue, hands that kill the innocent, a heart that plots evil, feet that race to do wrong, a false witness who pours out lies, and for one to sow discord in a family."* He hates those things, and we can feel hate for those things too.

But WHO does it say He hates? No one. He doesn't want a single person to be lost. He will chase them to the gates of hell to get them into heaven. He will forgive them of all their sin if they repent and turn to Him. However, He hates what was done to you.

He also hates to see the bitterness, pain, and suffering that unforgiveness is doing to you today. He hates the discord the bitterness is causing in your family. He hates the discord it is causing in His family of believers.

He wants us to forgive because He wants us free. He has a plan and a purpose that will give you joy and excitement about your life again. But you have no room for it if you are filled up with unforgiveness.

Forgiveness does not mean you think what was done to you was okay. It doesn't mean you have to act like it never happened. It happened, and it was bad. You didn't deserve it, and it hurt. The person who hurt you has no excuse that can make what they did right. If they have never acknowledged the wrong and apologized to you, it leaves you feeling diminished. All of that is wrong.

Your Father agrees with those statements. He said, "Vengeance is mine." He said that so you could know He isn't removing consequences for the sin done to you. It's just that He loves you far too much to let what was done to you in darkness leave a shadow on your soul and turn you into a hater. You aren't damaged; you are hurt. Let him heal your hurt and restore you to the person He created you to be.

It is always hurt people who hurt other people. The person who hurt you may have generations of hurts that have shaped and molded them into the hurtful person they became. Is that what you want to happen in your life? Is that the generational legacy you want to follow you?

Choosing unforgiveness is like repeatedly stabbing our own heart, yet wanting it to hurt the other person. Forgiveness doesn't make what was done right; it stops our bleeding, sets us free, and rightly aligns us with God.

You don't have to do this alone. Call on Holy Spirit and ask for the consuming fire of His love and truth to come and burn off all the unforgiveness so your heart can be softened and filled with spiritual joy that can only come from your salvation.

SCRIPTURE STUDY
MERCY GAINED.
MERCY GIVEN?

Psalm 103:8-12

Matthew 6:14-15; 18: 21-35

Luke 5:20; 6:37

Romans 8:1-2   2 Corinthians 5:18

Ephesians 4:31-32   Colossians 3:13

Focus: Whose Child?

One person that is hard to forgive is ourselves. If you are struggling with something you did in your past and holding on to shame, regret, and remorse, now is the right time to ask Holy Spirit why you can't forgive yourself.

Forgiving yourself doesn't mean you didn't make a mistake, commit a sin, or cause pain in someone else's life. It doesn't mean you have a good and valid excuse. It does mean that God loves you and that He is not condemning you. *"So now there is no condemnation for those who belong to Christ Jesus. And because you belong to him, the power of the life-giving Spirit has freed you from the power of sin that leads to death."*

He loves you and wants you to come close to Him. He has set you free from all that is in the past. He is asking you to come into Holy Spirit's presence, let the consuming fire burn off the regret and remorse, and accept the forgiveness freely offered to you.

This is not a question about whether you deserve forgiveness or not. It is simply a question of whether you want to live set free from this so God can restore the life He wants you to have.

Visualize you condemning yourself. Imagine you are standing in the middle of a path that leads to all God has for you. Instead of going toward all the good things in your future, you are facing back down the road to your past. As you stand on the path, you are preventing yourself from the good things God planned for your life. Imagine if God saw this scenario. He would say, "That is my child you are stopping. I have not condemned my child, so why are you? Will you please let my child go?" What would you say to God?

Step off of the path that leads to the death of your hopes and dreams; take a step toward the life He wants for you. Choose forgiveness and life.

HEARTWORK

After prayer and time in the presence of God, write out what He has shown you.

Discover

What has He revealed to you about unforgiveness in your heart?

Have you discovered why you can't forgive?

Make a list of people you haven't forgiven and why.

If you haven't forgiven yourself, list what you have done that you haven't forgiven yourself for.

Define

How has unforgiveness affected your life?

Do you feel bitterness? If you do, is it only toward a specific person, or has it spread to contaminate other areas of your life?

What do you think offering forgiveness to the people on your list would be saying about what happened?

Ask Jesus to show you what forgiving would mean.

What would change in your life if you did forgive?

Ask Jesus what He wants to say to you about your situation.

Defeat

Ask Jesus to show you how He sees the situation that caused the unforgiveness.

Ask Him for any revelations about the other person He wants to give you.

Ask Him about His vengeance.

Ask Holy Spirit to comfort you and strengthen you to do the will of God.

ONE VICTOR'S VOICE
FOR GOODNESS SAKE

Forgiveness was something I had given voice to many times. But even when I was parroting Jesus' words, *"Father, forgive them for they know not what they do,"* deep in my soul, I harbored hidden thoughts. *"Yes, they did know what they were doing. I did not deserve what happened to me. I was the one left to walk in despair. I lived covered in shame that they should wear. They don't seem to have suffered any consequences from their actions."* These and other obviously "un-Christian" thoughts ran through my soul.

Whenever I heard a sermon teaching that forgiveness is a decision we must make because Jesus chose to forgive us, I would tighten my resolve. My oft-repeated litany, "I will forgive them, I will forgive them," took on the cadence and pace of "the little train that could" phrase, "I think I can, I think I can." I would then shush the cry for justice that kept springing up in my heart, at least for a while.

I just couldn't rectify the idea that I had been the victim, and any court of law in America would mete out punishment to them. Yet here in Christiandom, I felt guilty for thinking those thoughts. My breakthrough came when I could longer manage the tension between what I heard from the pulpit, read from my Savior's words, and the cry for justice that kept echoing in my soul. I needed to know if He cared about what they did to me.

What I honestly wanted was justice. I wanted them to suffer because they made me suffer. I wanted to hold court; I could testify endlessly about the depth of the abuse, the betrayal, public shame and humiliation, the physical pain, the ridicule, and the demeaning way I was treated. I could also judge them. They were horribly wrong to mistreat an innocent. I could find every one of them guilty. And I could sentence them. They had no right to live their life as if I had never mattered, to never acknowledge the pain they had caused; they had to be held accountable.

In the moments spent getting honest about what was in my heart, Jesus was right there with me. He knew. He understood, yet He asked me to transfer all of that out of my heart by giving it to Him. *"Vengeance is Mine."* He said; I nodded. *"Forgiveness is Mine to give."* "Yes!" I agreed. *"Redemption is my heartbeat."* That caused me to pause.

Jonah wouldn't go to Nineveh because he knew if he told them about God, they would turn to Him and be redeemed. I understood how Jonah felt. I prayed hard about that. God didn't want anyone to be lost. I knew I had hurt other people because of the hurt done to me. Perhaps those who hurt me had done what they did because of what people had done to them. Could that be what was behind their action?

What would happen if I took them out of the courtroom in my heart and gave them over to God's courtroom? Could I release them to God, knowing He would save them if possible?

A realization came and brought Light; if He saved them, they would be changed. None of us can meet Him and not be changed. With Him in their heart, they would feel sorry for what they had done. They would know I mattered. There would be justice. Finally, slowly, thoughtfully, my response came. "So be it, I will let You finish this, Lord."

As I gave them to Him, He set my soul free. *"It is finished,"* He said. The darkness fell off my life, and I felt peace for the first time ever.

PART 9

NEW LOOK - ETERNAL VISION

FORGED IN FIRE EXCERPT:

"Long ago, in Vietnam, I dreamed I would become a general who fought to defend and bring freedom to the people of my country. God showed me that in my position with this ministry, I continually fight to defend all people's rights to have access to the Bible. There will always be true freedom in the country of my birth because Jesus has sent His Spirit into the people's hearts."

This excerpt is from Pastor Dan Dang's life story. As a young man, he dreamed of becoming a general in Vietnam. The situation in his war-torn country forced his family to evacuate. In a long, harrowing escape down a river and into the ocean, he watched as his country, the only life he had known, and his heart-held dream slipped from his life and disappeared.

When trauma invades our lives, it can seem to bring death to our life-long dreams. Many of you may have held a dream in your heart for years. Sometimes it seems to be just out of reach, around the next corner, or at the top of the next hill. There are times when trauma so drastic comes into your life that your dream is shattered.

It may have been a dream that would have been a very good thing. If you had accomplished your dream, you could have done good things. Good dreams, however, are not necessarily God-dreams. The Bible contains many incidences where dreams are given and fulfilled. There are also stories of delayed dreams and ones that change. We read that God gives dreams, comes to people in dreams, and helps people interpret their dreams and other people's dreams.

The excerpt reveals that Pastor Dan's story did not die. His heart desired to help his fellow countrymen be set free so they could live good lives. God used the desire behind the dream to direct him to the plan and the purpose He had for him from the time he created him.

The young boy leaving his country on that boat thought his dream was dead. God knew it wasn't. Everything that happened in Dan's life prepared him to fulfill his ultimate destiny. He encountered roadblocks along the way but never came to a dead-end. He had to let go of the lesser dream he had imagined so that God could bring into fulfillment the greater dream He had.

"Delight yourself also in the Lord, *and He shall give you the desires of your heart."* When we first read Psalm 37:4, there is often an immature understanding that causes us to create a dream based on the things of the world rather than the things of God. If we see our friend with a shiny new car, we could interpret this verse to mean that if we continue to delight in all the things of God, He will give us a shiny new car too.

As we walk with Jesus, embrace His ways in our lives, and learn more about His nature and character, however, we find that He begins to change the desire in our hearts. The things of earth grow dim, and the things of the kingdom grow ever brighter. He gives us desires in our hearts that will produce eternal outcomes.

When the young Vietnamese boy saw the atrocities and felt the pain in his country, he dreamed of being able to save the people of his country. His heart was given a desire from God for the people of his country to be saved. He ached for them to know freedom. The desire was formed in his heart, but the way to fulfill the desire was shaped by the frame of reference held in his mind. He saw strong, brave military generals leading the troops to bring freedom. From that viewpoint, he thought that would be the purpose of his life, so he planned to be a general.

God protected the desire He had given him. It wasn't a desire that would pass away with the change of government, be defeated by stronger people who had more weapons, or even a change of countries.

As his life unfolded, Pastor Dan was equipped with knowledge, skills, and experiences that seemed unrelated to his dream. He could not see they were part of God bringing forth the dream he thought was dead. When God knew Dan was ready to see with spiritual eyes, he opened the door to kingdom service.

He placed the desire to bring the Bible into Vietnam and other oppressed countries in his heart and began to connect him to ways to achieve the dream.

The desire given to the young boy had God's life breathed back into it, and it has brought forth a greater work in the kingdom than could have ever been accomplished in worldly work. Had he become a Lieutenant General, he would have commanded between twenty thousand to forty-five thousand troops.

The greater dream God has brought to life has allowed Pastor Dan the honor of seeing over one hundred thousand Vietnamese become Bible students. There are over eighty thousand students in thirty-seven other countries. Having seen God bring this dream into reality has shown him to dream big for God since He desires to do big things through us all.

If sadness has settled in your soul over a seemingly dead dream, seek your Father. He wants to give you a new understanding of the source of the desire in your heart.

If you hold a vision of your dream built around your frame of reference, God wants to show you that His ways are higher than ours. His thoughts are higher. Ask Him what He thinks about your shattered dream. Ask Him if He wants to breathe life back into any pieces of it. If not, ask Him if He will give you a new desire to hold in your heart that He wants to bring forth.

He has a plan and a purpose; seek diligently for it because it holds eternal blessings and joy for you.

SCRIPTURE STUDY:
WHOSE DREAM IS
IN YOUR HEART?

Psalm 105:16-21

1 Kings 3:3-15

Psalms 19:14; 139:23-24

Romans 15:21-29

Focus: Character for Destiny

Joseph's life journey was filled with dreams, and each impacted his life significantly. He is often labeled as "Joseph, the dreamer" in storybooks about his life. His story begins in Genesis 37. As always, the Scriptures have deep lessons, and abiding truths explained when we study Joseph. He was given two dreams when he was a young boy that he interpreted as meaning he would rise up to rule over his brothers.

Joseph was the favored child whose father's preference for him caused great discord in the family. (Something we know God hates) The young boy used his dreams to cause even more disharmony with his brothers, which caused them to plot to get rid of him. His pride got him dumped into a pit.

The focused Scripture tells of Joseph's many trials on his way to seeing the dream in his heart fulfilled in a way God intended from the beginning. *Until the time came to fulfill his dreams, the Lord tested Joseph's character."*

When He did rise up and rule, it was for the good of God's people, all of them, including the brothers, who had intended harm for Joseph. Because he relied on God to bring the dream to fruition, he handled his brothers in an honorable way.

If Joseph had failed the tests that came year after year, he would not have seen his dream fulfilled, and there would have been great kingdom loss. During his journey, he went from a favored child to a slave, to a house servant for Pharoah, a prisoner, and finally, he became a great leader. None of that journey fit the way he thought the dream would happen.

With every incident, he had the opportunity to abandon the dream. He could have turned to the things of the world and satisfied his flesh, but he didn't. God kept using dreams to let him know He was still with him. As long as God kept talking to him, Joseph kept doing the next thing God asked of him. Joseph, because of his good character, fulfilled God's dream.

God also went to Solomon in a dream. He gave him a very intriguing option. God said, "What do you want? Ask, and I will give it to you!" Imagine the God of the universe asking what you want. It was a blank check.

What answer springs to your mind? Solomon's response is from a place of awe and wonder because of his great love of God and compassion for the people of God. He said, *"Give to Your servant an understanding heart to judge Your people, that I may discern between good and evil. For who is able to judge this great people of Yours?"* God had appointed him as judge over the people, and he wanted to fulfill the tasks he had been given well.

Jesus has brought salvation to the earth, and He is the judge of all. Solomon's desire for wisdom because of compassion for people and his desire to serve the Lord is a foundational attitude we need so we can see God's dreams fulfilled through our lives. God's dream given to our hearts shows us our mission; our attitude and character will determine how we handle the tasks require to fulfill that mission.

The healing work you have been doing through these pages is part of your journey to your destiny. Letting the consuming fire of Holy Spirit burn off the lies you have believed, the labels you have put on yourself and others, and the limitations you have allowed to restrict your life makes room for your dream's fulfillment.

In Proverbs 13 we find, *"It is pleasant to see dreams come true, but fools refuse to turn from evil to attain them."* One of the meanings of a fool is "a person who is victimized or duped." If you have been convinced by the enemy of your soul that the lies, labels, and limitations are true, you are being duped.

It is time to draw close to God and ask Holy Spirit to show you the dream He has for you. God wants you to fulfill it even more than you do. He has great and wonderful things for you to do in the kingdom the way that only you can do. It is bigger than you know. He is asking today if you will let go of the lesser dream you have had so He can fulfill His greater dream through you.

HEARTWORK

*After prayer and time in the presence of God, write
out what He has shown you.*

Discover

What has He revealed about a dream you have held in
your heart which hasn't happened yet?

Do you know what that dream means to you; what lies
behind the dream?

Pastor Dan dreamed of being a general, not for power
and control, but to bring freedom to his countrymen.
What does your heart want from your dream?

If God spoke to you and said, "What do you want?"
What would your answer be? Why?

Define

What have you come to believe from any unfulfilled
dreams?

If your dream has been shattered, ask God what He
has to say to you about the dream.

Ask God for His dream for your life. Spend time
seeking His vision and the ways He wants to fulfill it.

Defeat

Ask Holy Spirit to reveal everything in your heart preventing you from seeking God's plan and purpose.

Make a list and continually seek Him for Scripture to guide you in overcoming whatever is not of Him.

Until you have comfort and peace about your dream, sincerely pray Psalm 19:14,

"May the words of my mouth, and the meditation of my heart, be pleasing to you, O Lord, my rock and my redeemer."

Seek His response to Psalm 139:23-24, *"Search me, O God, and know my heart; test me and know my anxious thoughts. Point out anything in me that offends you, and lead me along the path of everlasting life."*

ONE VICTOR'S VOICE
SHOP FOR HOPE

My playroom was all set up; I had everything in place and ready for the shoppers. Every scrap of my art supplies had been transformed into treasures I was sure people would want. I had prices on each piece, and the cash register from under my Christmas tree was ready for action.

My family was summoned, and my neighborhood friends got sales flyers regularly. There was rarely a time in my life when I didn't replay this scenario. I dreamed of the shop I would have one day. It would be magnificent and make me "the richest girl in the west," I often told anyone who would listen to my dream.

After finishing college, I worked in retail for many years and finally opened my shop offering hand-poured candles, melt-and-pour soap, and jewelry creations I made from natural stones and gems. I planned to add a line of home décor when I could find the time. Since I had a tight budget, the space I rented was not in the best part of town.

There was a recovery halfway house next door, and I was constantly bumping into someone from there. At first, I didn't know how to talk to or act around them. Then I met Janie. She had gone to the same high school I had, and we had some friends in common. She began to open up to me about what her life had been like. Broken family life had left her alone and unwanted. Alcohol and drugs had been her only comfort. She talked a lot about letting go of it all and letting God work out the details of her life. She couldn't find a job since drug use had ruined her job references.

I loved my shop but couldn't keep up with all the work. I was always exhausted and knew I was missing opportunities to develop my products and promote my business. I had begun to think about selling the inventory and returning to work for someone else so they could do the worrying.

If this is my dream, why am I so miserable? This thought kept running through my head, but I simply did not have time to answer it. But God did.

For three nights in a row, I dreamed that my shop was filled with beautiful things, but I knew none of them were made by me. As I began to ask Him for wisdom, He began to highlight Scripture. Ecclesiastes 4:9, *Two people are better off than one, for they can help each other succeed,"* sent the feeling of an electric shock through my body.

I knew what was missing from my dream. I longed for others to share and help develop the dream God had given me. Instantly, I thought of the girls from next door. He was showing me we could help each other succeed.

Interestingly, when I left my prayer chair that morning, I knocked an old journal off the shelf next to me. It fell open onto the floor, and when I picked it up, I saw where I had written, *Teamwork Makes the Dream Work*, by John Maxwell. That caused me to laugh aloud.

My shop is magnificent now, and it includes a coffee shop area. It provides well for me, and my job brings me so much joy that it is hard to describe.

When I see these girls who come work with me grow and become the women God wanted them to be because they found hope again, I know His dream for this shop has made me the "richest girl in the west."

PART 10

YOUR STORY

"That day in her hospital room, I was strengthened for what was ahead. God had given me the powerful sense that it was time for me to go to Brenda. God placed me in the parking lot at precisely the same time the nurse walked by my parking space because that was part of His plan. She opened the way for me to get to Brenda's side to connect with her while she could still communicate."

" I have told you all this so that you may have peace in me. Here on earth, you will have many trials and sorrows. But take heart, because I have overcome the world." Jesus talked about many things with His disciples before He left the earth. This verse shows His heart for His followers because He doesn't want us to be caught off guard when trouble comes our way.

He had lived in close relationships with these disciples. He knew they had great faith, but only He knew what they were about to go through. Being with Him had given them a new dream in their hearts and hope for a much better future.

Their thinking had been transformed since they had glimpsed a heavenly way of life. But now, He was headed to the cross, knowing they would be troubled by other people. He didn't want them to lose the peace He gave them during their time together.

His message to them that day is for us today; he said it was for all that would come to believe because of those first disciples. As you have drawn closer and have experienced healing and renewed hope for your future, He doesn't want you to lose your peace when another round of trouble comes.

Many of the outward circumstances of our lives will be the same for a while longer. The world is still broken, and we all still have an enemy of our soul who wants nothing better than to attempt to discredit the Truth you have been shown in this work. Our Father is sovereign, however, and He will never waiver in His love for His children.

When trouble comes, fix your eyes on Jesus. Remember the Scriptures He has placed in your mind. Speak aloud the Truth you heard about who you are, and stand firm in your faith in Him. You are His child forever. Trust Him to finish the good work He has started in you. None of us can endure hardships alone; we must rely entirely on Jesus and everything He has taught us.

When Jesus told the adulterous woman whom He refused to condemn to "go and sin no more," it was a statement showing her that she was not a helpless victim of sin. He knew she could turn from the past, follow His Words and ways, and live differently.

His faith in her is an encouraging reminder that He sees us and knows we are stronger than we think we are. He doesn't expect any of us to be perfect, but He knows we can reach for righteousness with a heart that wants to be worthy of His work on the cross that saved us from hell. He sent Holy Spirit to help strengthen us and bring truth to our minds.

He cares about every detail of our lives. *"The LORD directs the steps of the godly. He "*inclines toward*" every detail of their lives. Though they stumble, they will never fall, for the LORD holds them by the hand."* This truth is apparent in the middle of Dave's most painful situation. The excerpt from his book found here reflects on that time. His wife, co-laborer, helper, and soul mate was in the hospital during COVID.

This Scripture is usually translated as "He delights in every detail." This was not a situation God delighted in, but the understanding of the Hebrew word used here is, "He inclines, or leans toward" every detail. He knew the pain Dave was in and what the outcome would be.

Brenda had been rushed to a hospital whose rules prevented Dave from seeing her. God knew Dave needed time with her and opened the way for that to happen. He held Dave in His hand and directed every step. It was a precious act of Dave's Father to help Dave see Brenda again before she left the earth.

Dave's faith was never shaken. He felt the Father with him and journeyed through the hard goodbye, still submitted and committed to God's plan for his life. The grief was powerful; however, the strength of God was even greater and carried him through the pain. Because of the healing work Dave had done with God while Brenda was at his side, he knew whose child Brenda was. He also knew he belonged to Him. There was never a doubt that he would see Brenda again.

In deep grief and sorrow, Dave could have stopped the ministry he was called to do. He never considered it. He has continued to travel and speak to people to share the good news of Jesus and the salvation and healing He offers to all.

The strength, comfort, and courage God showered on him during this time of grief increased his desire to reach other people with God's message. He knows he couldn't have gotten through this loss without God. His compassion for others compels him to let them know Jesus is there for them, too. He is still telling his story because it is the story of God working through him every moment of his life.

There is a moment in our souls when we know we are standing at an important point in our journey. This text has focused on healing the soul.

During the work, there has been an open discussion about emotions affected by trauma. The thoughts based on lies instead of truth have been revealed. Each exercise has encouraged prayer and time with the presence of God to bring transformation. Now it is time to strengthen and refocus our will. This is a point of decision that can determine the rest of your story.

Each chapter has contained a "victor's voice" section relating a story of a person who stepped out of the past trauma and strongholds and reclaimed the life God had planned. Each person had a story shaped and defined by what had happened to them.

Each one, however, came to a point in their journey and decided to trust in God with all their heart. They decided they no longer wanted to trust what trauma said about them. They refused to let trauma from the past define who they are today. They strengthened their will to let go of the past and let God direct their path. Step by step, He led them as their true destiny unfolded.

Strengthening our will begins with prayer. Ask God to strengthen your will. Ask to be shown how God wants you to focus your will. We all must admit that patterns of thought and entrenched emotions are still being overcome. We can ask Him to help us overcome the old and turn to the new life He has planned for us.

Chapter 11 of Luke's gospel recorded a time when Jesus was teaching about prayer. Jesus said, "And so I tell you, keep on asking, and you will receive what you ask for. Keep on seeking, and you will find. Keep on knocking, and the door will be opened to you. For everyone who asks, receives. Everyone who seeks finds. And to everyone who knocks, the door will be opened.

You fathers, if your children ask for a fish, do you give them a snake instead? Or do you give them a scorpion if they ask for an egg? Of course not! So, if you sinful people know how to give good gifts to your children, how much more will your heavenly Father give the Holy Spirit to those who ask him."

Persist in your prayers for a will that wills to do the will of God. Also, notice that He said the good gift from the Father is the Holy Spirit. Ask for a refreshing of Holy Spirit in your soul every day.

Mark 9 revealed an incident when a father brought his son to Jesus for healing. The boy had been tormented for years. He was bound for so long that it was deeply entrenched. The disciples had not been able to help. The father begged Jesus for help, saying, "Help us, if you can."

"What do you mean, 'If I can?" Jesus asked. *"Anything is possible if a person believes."* The father instantly cried out, *"I do believe, but help me overcome my unbelief!"*

Some days, those things you have believed for so long may seem truer than what the Lord has said to you. On those days, the boy's father's words may also be your heart's cry. The good news is that Jesus is right there. Stand on your decision to trust Him; He will strengthen your faith if you ask.

"For I know the thoughts that I think toward you, says the LORD, thoughts of peace and not of evil, to give you a future and a hope. After John 3:16, Jeremiah 29:11 is perhaps the most well-known verse of the Bible. The context is that God's people are in bondage in a foreign place. That is symbolic of living a life in bondage to the aftermath of trauma. But God says He will bring them back to Him. The way back for them is the way back for us all. He says when you turn back to me, *"You will call upon Me and go and pray to Me, and I will listen to you. And you will seek Me and* **find Me when you search for Me with all your heart."**

Our souls must be cleansed of the old to make room for nothing but His truth about who we are and His plans for us. Are you wholeheartedly ready to seek Him and leave all the old things in the past?

HEARTWORK

The revelations you have gained as you "Discovered, Defined, and Defeated" anything in your soul preventing you from drawing closer to God revealed important information.

The day we are born, we become disciples of the world. The first meaning of the word disciple is "learner." From the world, we all learn our identities defined by worldly terms. The "heartwork" in this guide has revealed what you have learned. When we meet Jesus and accept Him as Lord of our lives, it is an opportunity to become His disciple so we can learn from Him. The call on our lives is clear and simple. He says, *"Come, follow Me."*

It is an offer that few will answer. Sometimes it seems impossible to be a disciple because we think we must be able to do it all right and perfectly. When we understand that disciple means "learner," it changes our perspective. Learners have teachers who invest time in helping them understand a little better, get a little stronger, and achieve a little more every day.

We learned about Paul's journey to becoming an apostle. In his letter to the church at Philippi, he shared the way he looked at it. *"I press on to possess that perfection for which Christ Jesus first possessed me. No, dear brothers and sisters, I have not achieved it, but I focus on this one thing: Forgetting the past and looking forward to what lies ahead, I press on to reach the end of the race and receive the heavenly prize for which God, through Christ Jesus, is calling us.*

What will your soul answer? Will you follow Him to become a lifelong learner of His Ways?

ONE VICTOR'S VOICE
YOUR STORY

When your soul is healed, and you are becoming the person He created you to be, your voice will be raised to tell of His love and power. Your voice will stir others to want more of Him in their lives. Your voice will be used to shatter the darkness and bring light and hope to the oppressed.

"He has made everything beautiful in its time. Also, He has put eternity in their hearts, except that no one can find out the work that God does from beginning to end." We won't fully understand until we get to heaven that there was a purpose to your pain and beauty in the scars.

However, the very fabric of our being is aware of a sense of longing in our hearts for the eternal things of God. We touch the eternal part of others' hearts by sharing what He has done for us. That bond gives us a greater view of God's work in the world.

This is that point on your journey when you choose the direction you will go. That choice will determine the rest of your story.

Be strong and courageous, and never forget that He is with you on every step of this journey.

ABOUT PEGGY CORVIN

Author, freedom minister, speaker, and teacher, Peggy Corvin has a passion for bringing freedom to believers. She obtained a Master's degree in theology from The King's University to deepen her understanding of Scripture and ways to help share the power of the Word of God to break strongholds.

Her personal story is found in *Diamond in the Darkness: Abused Child of Darkness, Reclaimed Daughter of Light.* She has had the honor of co-authoring several books, including John and Angel Arroyo's story and devotional, *Get Up! Get Up!* You can also find her on Audible, as narrator of a variety of books. She and her husband, Stan Corvin, own Southwestern Legacy Press, where they help others bring their stories to the world.

Made in the USA
Monee, IL
15 April 2024

56722230R00069